List Your Self

Listmaking as the Way to Self-Discovery

Ilene Segalove • Paul Bob Velick

Andrews McMeel
Publishing®

www.andrewsmcmeel.com

Andrews McMeel Publishing, LLC

an Andrews McMeel Universal company

1130 Walnut Street, Kansas City, Missouri 64106

www.andrewsmcmeel.com

ISBN: 978-1-4494-1145-9

Dedicated to my parents, Elaine and Milton Segalove.

Her zest for listmaking inspires.

His ability to live well sans list amazes.

To their continued love of doing.

Paper or not.

—Ilene Segalove

Dedicated to my mother, Dorinne Velick,

and to my father, Stuart Velick,

who each listed a great life day-in-and-day-out

no matter the time or the territory.

—Paul Bob Velick

CONTENTS

Introduction vii

How to Use This Book xv

Yourself 1
preferences • heroic feats • fears
loves • regrets • laughs • tears

Daily Life 37
friends • home • errands • frustrations • stuff
transportation • technology • communications • garbage

Business 65
deals • risks • lawsuits • headaches • bosses
jobs • money • schemes • success

Change 95
surprise • growth • higher purpose • touchstones
fun • stupidity • mentors • wins • losses

Culture 123
ecology • politics • movies • history • anarchy
song • space • fashion • sports

Men and Women 153
love • sex • romance • acts of passion • terms
fantasies • lies • promises • heartaches

Greater Truths 187
values • happiness • courage • meaning • death
trust • God • luck • fear • wonderment

Health 211
potions • food • body parts • stress • routines
regimes • longevity • sleep • ailments

Growing Up 243
favorite things • home • school • magic • parents
games • lessons • fads • secrets • heroes • ghosts

Suddenly . . . 269
fantasy • time travel • immortality • dreams come true
big bucks • superpowers

Introduction

For some reason, we love to ignore who or what we really are. But being truly human and liking it requires self-knowledge. It gives our experience resonance. It lends a vibe, an echo, a wholeness to what we think and feel. Self-knowledge is fun. It leads to wonderment, personal investigation, and new discoveries. It opens up the cracks and lets loose the bits and pieces of ourselves we haven't met . . . yet.

List Your Self unlocks the door to your personal identity. It's an easy, provocative, and liberating opportunity to get to know yourself. At first, the idea of jotting down a list seems almost too mundane, just another task to get done. But once you start, you'll suddenly discover an inventory of personal secrets, fears, and desires that flow out effortlessly and surprise you. There you are, big as life, in list form.

Listmaking gives us the tools for being seen. Listmaking gives us the strategy for being heard. Listmaking is the road from unknowing to knowing. No guru necessary. No therapist. No special diet. No need to suffer. Memories deep in your consciousness will emerge to fill in the blanks. All you need is a pen or pencil, a solid moment, and *List Your Self*. Remember "Know thyself"? Try "List thyself."

You may wonder, "Do I really need a new diary, another journal?" Are you already a blank-book junkie? Got one started and then just had to buy the new red corduroy version? *List Your Self* is not just another journal. And it's not exactly blank. The list suggestions coax you into revealing your deepest thoughts. Can this be journaling? Sure, if you want to call it that. But journaling can be a little bit lonesome. *List Your Self* headings provide triggers, topical suggestions to take you on your pilgrimage and keep you company. And by simply listmaking, you'll learn instantly what you love, what you can't live without, what drives you crazy, and how to prioritize all the pieces of your busy life.

Like a journal, the meat (or tofu) and potatoes of this book is your daily grind, grist for the mill of your evolution and entertainment. And, like journaling, listmaking is a soulful, solitary act. But listmaking is journaling at its best. It gives you the chance to complete a task. When you journal, you make entry after entry after entry. There's no closure in sight. *List Your Self* actually has a happy ending. There are no wrong answers. And every time you finish a list, you finish a huge thought, pull up a big memory, and dive into or put to rest a major psychological story.

For example, "List all the ways you tried to make your father happy." Did you ever really make him happy? Then you gaze out the window for a moment and remember his beaming face the time you:

- Got 100 percent on the geometry final
- Used the word "may" instead of "can" in a complete sentence
- Wore a bathing cap in the pool without being told
- Put his big scissors back on the silver hook in the workshop where they belonged
- Always asked a question, even if it sounded stupid
- Gave him a necktie with little drawings of chemistry equations
- Ate Roquefort cheese on crackers, even though it tasted awful, because it felt bad to see him eat alone

Memory lane and then some. The very process of writing and then reading that "dad" list might open a peephole from your brain straight into your soul. It could access layers of feelings and colors and sensations and even give you a little sense of well-being. It doesn't hurt to eke out the answers, and it won't take much energy or courage, just the willingness to poke around a little.

The archaic root of "list" means "listen to." To what? Eavesdrop on yourself. All day long, you are busy whispering all kinds of things to yourself. Grab that ongoing dialogue and put it in a list. Do some personal eavesdropping. You'll be glad you did.

And what about being "listless"? Having or being of no interest, because of weariness or illness or spiritlessness or dejection or having no *List Your Self* to write in? Having no lists is list-less. How easily remedied— just pick up a pencil and you are on-line, on time, and officially alive.

Remember, you are not obligated to pour out your heart, record your day, do seasonal reviews of your judgments, relationships, or state of health. *List Your Self* encourages you to take stock of your life in a far less threatening way. *List Your Self* is a poultice. It draws out things you never knew were there. Spit it out. Tidy up your act. *List Your Self* is a magnet. It pulls you ahead of yourself so you can gaze from a distance and see your life's landscape. In the process, it gives you a chance to drop anchor, and explore safely. You will feel like a well-equipped tourist investigating your personal landscape. And the payoff is huge. It's a coming home. You may actually discover you like where you live. You may end up feeling more at ease, in a psychological and physical space that's not only bigger and better than you ever imagined but delightfully familiar as well.

There is something profound that happens in the making of a list. It goes beyond the obvious enumeration of stuff you need to get done. For example, take "List all the stuff you gotta do today."

- Pick up resoled shoes
- Test phone machine again
- Find a box of barbecued pig's ears for the dog
- Call Mom
- Kill snails
- Return tuxedo
- Write IRS

Now try "List all the times you've experienced something remarkable in your life."

Simply reading those words energizes a whole set of responses that are far more stimulating than "List all the stuff you gotta do today." It's almost like the difference between eating a mud pie and a fresh hot apple turnover.

Listmaking is an elegant, complete, and artful act in and of itself. The very process is a breakthrough change of mind. To "List all the times you've experienced something remarkable in your life" begins an instant journey of exploration and wonder. Simply having been asked to consider creates a repertoire of items that are uniquely you. Say hello to yourself. The true listee is waking up.

Okay, so it feels a little uncomfortable at first. Even frustrating. How do you access these answers? Where do they live? How do you get into listing mode? In a minute you might feel a list coming through, but the words are stuck in a distant mind folder with no identifiable title in view. Eventually you discover a puzzle piece, don't quite know where it fits, and then— "Ahhh. . . . Wasn't that Uncle Lou who pulled my lost pearl necklace out of his shoe in 1965? Yes, that was remarkable. And Little Danny Wrigley got a weird feeling that day in October when we stood under a tree on the top of Tower Hill and he screamed, 'Run, as fast as you can!'—and in seconds the tree was hit by lightning and exploded and we were safe!" My life *has* had its remarkable moments! That's two of them.

"List all the phone calls that changed your life." Hmmmm . . . The call from my sister when she found an old photo of me doing a cartwheel and winning an award in a tumbling contest didn't change my life. Not really. But wait. I never knew I could do anything like that. I was a clod, wasn't I? What happened? And the letter from the IRS about them owing me $5,000 wasn't a life changer, really, but I bought a telescope with the refund and saw Halley's comet, and that got me interested in becoming a part-time astronomer, which gave my life more meaning. Do letters count?

Don't worry. This is not a psychological profile. Not a personal evaluation system. No tests. No final scores at the end of the book. No board of experts telling you if your life story is worthwhile; of course it is. This is simply a wild and probing ride through your personal history. Put on the miner's hat with the light and sharpen your pick. Dig in. Dig deep. There's gold in them thar hills.

Listmaking turns on the juices. Your memory will start to dance. It's a bit like reaching into last night's dream to grab that image or sensation that made you feel so happy in the morning. It's an exercise that flexes a muscle you may not have used in a while. And then, if you're lucky, a hint. Say it was George Clooney in last night's dream. Now you've got something to work with. One thing on your list leads to another. It's contagious, like a roomful of yawners. Listmaking works the same way as dream connection. If you can just find the road, the scent, the George Clooney, you can get into list suggestion. And once in, you're on. Relax. Lists happen.

Our minds are habit formers. We forget how to think in more than a few limiting ways. Patterns work but patterns repeat. What's new? Lists keep us shifting and growing. So if you read on page 271 of *List Your Self*, "Suddenly you've been granted lunch with God; list your grievances," what do you do? Do you consider where you two might be dining? Is God a vegetarian? Can you even bother with this kind of list suggestion after the busy day you've had? What if, for even one second, you did try to whip out a few responses. You might find a certain glee in hosting such an off-the-wall proposal. "Okay," you say, "I'm sitting with God. But I don't believe in God . . . I don't think." Such a stretch. What if you did? Pretend. "I don't pretend." But you did once? "Yes, I had an imaginary playmate named Fred, and we used to float on the ceiling and whisper into each other's ear." Get the point?

You pretended, once. You made up stories and dreamed and felt entitled—entitled to fun and open to the deep truths about life and yourself at the same time. Listmaking asks you to be that kid again. Except this time, more than likely, a kid with a vocabulary, preferences, strong opinions, and the desire to speak up and be heard. See yourself unedited. Political correctness out the window, please. Ignore the voices of the critic and editor and English 101 professor—they can slip right into your brain and tell you making a list is foolish. Don't listen. Just list.

We are all deep, dense, intricate resources of years of reactions and feelings and dreams. We house magic and creativity and vision, often embedded inside distorted daily routines and humdrum ways of thinking.

We remember only a fraction of who we are. Listmaking unknots these patterns. It is a natural human need to put it out there! Make a list and grow two inches.

Maybe you've got list phobia. Your mom and dad used to leave on a trip and The List would be taped on the refrigerator door, blasting orders, endless things to remember, reprimands, and warnings: "Don't drink out of the milk bottle! Puff the pillows on the velveteen couch every time you get off it! Don't dare go into our bedroom! Wipe your feet before walking on the orange carpet!" Lists were cruel, an ominous assignment hanging heavy before you. Just gazing at them hurt.

It was intense. But fortunately, you're not living that list anymore. Of course, even though you're in charge now, a few simple lists might get you running for cover. "List everything that's in your garage." Or "List all the fears you have when you wake up in the morning." Or "List all the possible things that could happen when you park in an underground structure." You don't want to think about this? Why look for trouble? Lighten up. Make a list. You'll get it all out and feel better for it. *List Your Self* might seem like a literary Pandora's box, and it is, but in the best sense. Full of life, good and bad. Full of you.

There can be joy in listmaking. And surprises. "List all the teachers you can remember and put a descriptive word next to each name." Try that one. Laugh out loud. Besides an onslaught of old faces, names, and places, you'll be hearing and remembering the old you. Just to think, *Fourth grade, Mrs. Freck/pale;* or *Sixth grade, Mr. Zink/crew cut;* or *Miss Shrimpee/not very shrimpy, gym teacher, made us run laps* dredges up images of odd-fitting gym suits and smells of red licorice hidden in the lockers. And there was Mr. Beck, the science teacher, who one day fainted over a lab table oozing sulfur and we had to get the school nurse.

Wouldn't it feel good to fill in "List all the smells that make you scream"?

- That very pretty Mrs. Fish, who used to bake the cafeteria cinnamon rolls and who wore too much perfume
- Freshly made cotton candy, so sweet it made your teeth hurt just to take a whiff

- All the main streets in New Zealand cities, bellowing out the heavy smell of pork cooking
- Rose gardens with so many roses in bloom you swoon
- Mr. Murphy at the hardware store
- The county fair
- Burning tar
- Uncle Herby's potato pancakes (scream with happiness!)

So you've filled in all the blanks. You've carried *List Your Self* around in your briefcase or in your car. It's your story now, page by page. You've written in it privately in bed, on the subway, at the red light, while talking on the phone. You've used it to recognize an important life passage, filling it in when you turned thirty or fifty, or in between jobs, or as a nightly ritual just before sleep. Now you get to read it.

List Your Self is a time capsule of who you are and where you've been. It's up to the minute. It's your latest snapshot. See your heart, mind, and soul lined up in one neat vertical row. And now that you've done it, your life will never look the same. You'll be more in touch, more agile. You'll feel liberated from the unspoken and the unwritten. You'll be able to tell better tales, crash through writer's block, make a million dollars, or maybe not. Don't fret. Self-knowledge is its own reward.

And remember, don't be fooled by the overwhelming feeling that some things are just too much, too heavy, too personal, too sacred to be listed. These are the Ultimate Lists, the ones you've prepared for. These are the ones you want to really engage in. These are the lists that crack the code and give entry into the stuff we're made of, like "List all the people who love you for who you really are" or "List the things you'd like to be remembered for when you die" or "List all the ways you've helped others." See, you've thought about this stuff now. You're accountable. You have listened deeply and discovered more than you ever imagined. Pat yourself on the back: Good work. Or, of course, fill in "List all the reasons you should congratulate and celebrate yourself."

HOW TO USE THIS BOOK

This is a book about you. *List Your Self* is also about the outside world and your relationship with it. The key to getting the most from it is understanding that it reflects your life in *this present* moment. The personal issues you bring to *List Your Self* in the morning will surely be different by afternoon or the next day. For this reason, it is important to read through the lists so the ones that touch you, speak to you, beg you to choose them will guide you in deciding what you should list right now.

Three Ways to Begin

1. Flip through the chapters. When a list idea pops out, go there. Choose three to seven topics this way and start listing. Or . . .
2. Attack at random, skipping here and there. Then make your own composite. Or . . .
3. Start from page one and move sequentially through. There's nothing wrong with order.

Write the answers in the book slowly, honestly. Keep it personal, confidential, and always write whatever comes to mind first. Try not to get stuck in your head.

Move to another list if you feel unsure. When your lists are finished, you may read your answers right away, or set them aside and review them at another time. The combined wisdom of the chosen batch of lists will illuminate the truth about whatever issues you brought today.

When to Use This Book

On your travels
Big birthdays
Upon waking
During career moves
At the outset of marriage
When you are troubled
At parties
Standing in long lines
When you are overwhelmed
When you feel stuck
When you forget your purpose in life
Before bed

Why Use This Book?

To get the chance for confession, without judgment
To shed light in dark personal areas
To take inventory of your sensibilities
For answers to personal questions
To learn about yourself
To remember your worth
To be surprised
To have fun
Why not?

The Authors' Five Favorite Lists at This Particular Sitting

1. List all the objects you wish you had from your parents' living room.
   That Herman Miller sunshine clock
   All those wooden ducks
   The John Martin print in the big cedar wood frame

All their record albums
The tobacco humidor
The brick dining room floor

2. List what usually goes through your mind just before you fall asleep.

The things humans choose to do
Wishing it were normal to sleep for sixteen hours
How much oxygen there is in the atmosphere
The things my friends do and say
Places in the world to build houses
What the Indians in the world are doing now
What if tomorrow there was no more metal on Earth
What keeps everyone from sleeping with one another

3. List all the greetings you've used to answer your telephone.

"Happy Anniversary"
"It's your dime"
"Taco Bell"
"Ed's pencil house, Steve speaking"
"Monday"
"This better be good"
"Carnaby Street"
"Situation Comedy"
"Mail room"

4. Suddenly your house is on fire; list the stuff you'd grab.

My grandfather's Rolleiflex camera
Some journals
Some old Guatemalan fabrics
As many paintings and small sculptures as I can carry
Some business folders
My German binoculars
My journals wrapped in those Guatemalan fabrics

My paintings and African guys wrapped in Balinese fabrics
My Germanic binoculars tied to some family pics and pens
My dad's shotgun and my mom's Peruvian vase stuffed
    with Picasso records
Family photos
My grandmother's exotic glasses case

5. List some of the people who have really changed your life.
Miles Davis
Igor Stravinsky
Andy Warhol
Krishnamurti
Frank Zappa
Billy Finbro
Dark Bob

YOURSELF

LIST ALL THE QUALITIES YOU LOVE ABOUT BEING HUMAN.

_____

_____

_____

_____

_____

_____

_____

_____

_____

_____

_____

_____

_____

_____

_____

_____

_____

_____

_____

_____

LIST ALL THE ACTIVITIES YOU'D DO IF YOU WEREN'T SO AFRAID.

LIST YOUR "SUNDAY" RITUALS.

LIST THE COMPLIMENTS YOU RECEIVE ON A REGULAR BASIS.

List the places you go in your mind when you want some peace and quiet.

LIST ALL THE THINGS YOU'VE MADE OR BUILT BY HAND.

_____

_____

_____

_____

_____

_____

_____

_____

_____

_____

_____

_____

_____

_____

_____

_____

_____

_____

_____

_____

LIST THE WAYS THE FULL MOON AFFECTS YOUR BEHAVIOR.

_____

_____

_____

_____

_____

_____

_____

_____

_____

_____

_____

_____

_____

_____

_____

_____

_____

_____

_____

_____

_____

LIST THE SITUATIONS THAT ALWAYS MAKE YOU CRY.

LIST YOUR FAVORITE TALENTS.

_____

_____

_____

_____

_____

_____

_____

_____

_____

_____

_____

_____

_____

_____

_____

_____

_____

_____

_____

_____

LIST ALL THE SMELLS THAT MAKE YOU SCREAM.

List all the names you've been called, endearing and not so.

_____

_____

_____

_____

_____

_____

_____

_____

_____

_____

_____

_____

_____

_____

_____

_____

_____

_____

_____

_____

_____

LIST HOW YOU FEEL WHEN YOU'VE BEEN LIED TO.

LIST WHAT ALWAYS MAKES YOU LAUGH.

LIST WHAT CONSISTENTLY WORRIES YOU EACH DAY.

LIST THE WAYS YOU DON'T CARE TO DIE.

_____

_____

_____

_____

_____

_____

_____

_____

_____

_____

_____

_____

_____

_____

_____

_____

_____

_____

_____

_____

LIST ANY TELEPATHIC OR PARANORMAL EXPERIENCES YOU'VE HAD.

LIST WHAT USUALLY GOES THROUGH YOUR MIND JUST BEFORE YOU FALL ASLEEP.

_____

_____

_____

_____

_____

_____

_____

_____

_____

_____

_____

_____

_____

_____

_____

_____

_____

_____

LIST THE ANIMALS THAT REALLY SCARE YOU.

_____

_____

_____

_____

_____

_____

_____

_____

_____

_____

_____

_____

_____

_____

_____

_____

_____

_____

_____

_____

_____

_____

LIST THE HEROIC FEATS YOU'VE PERFORMED.

LIST ALL THE PEOPLE YOU WISH YOU HADN'T TRUSTED.

LIST ALL THE PROMISES YOU KEEP MAKING TO YOURSELF.

LIST YOUR TYPICAL DAYDREAMS.

LIST WHAT YOU WISH WHENEVER YOU SEE A SHOOTING STAR, BLOW OUT YOUR BIRTHDAY CANDLES, OR DROP A COIN IN A FOUNTAIN.

_____

_____

_____

_____

_____

_____

_____

_____

_____

_____

_____

_____

_____

_____

_____

_____

_____

_____

_____

LIST ALL THE QUALITIES IN YOURSELF YOU LIKE THE LEAST.

List all the things you'd like to say to your mother.

_____

_____

_____

_____

_____

_____

_____

_____

_____

_____

_____

_____

_____

_____

_____

_____

_____

_____

_____

_____

_____

_____

_____

_____

List all the ways you tried to make your father happy.

_____

_____

_____

_____

_____

_____

_____

_____

_____

_____

_____

_____

_____

_____

_____

_____

_____

_____

_____

_____

_____

List the beauty tricks you perform to make you look "better."

LIST THE MEMORIES YOU'D LIKE TO FORGET.

_____

_____

_____

_____

_____

_____

_____

_____

_____

_____

_____

_____

_____

_____

_____

_____

_____

_____

_____

_____

_____

_____

_____

_____

LIST THE THINGS YOU HEAR YOURSELF SAY OUT LOUD DAY AFTER DAY.

LIST WHAT YOU LIKE TO DO WHEN YOU ARE ALONE.

LIST THE THINGS YOU'VE SAID THAT YOU'D LIKE TO TAKE BACK.

LIST ALL THE IMPORTANT PERSONAL NUMBERS YOU'VE
COMMITTED TO MEMORY.

LIST YOUR SELF

LIST ALL THE PEOPLE WHO LOVE YOU FOR WHO YOU REALLY ARE.

_____

_____

_____

_____

_____

_____

_____

_____

_____

_____

_____

_____

_____

_____

_____

_____

_____

_____

_____

_____

LIST ALL THE REASONS YOU SHOULD CONGRATULATE AND CELEBRATE YOURSELF.

DAILY LIFE

LIST ALL THE THINGS YOU HIDE WHEN YOUR FRIENDS COME TO VISIT.

List what's under your kitchen sink.

LIST WHAT KINDS OF PEOPLE SHOULD NEVER DRIVE CARS.

LIST THE THINGS YOU DO BETWEEN TURNING OFF THE ALARM AND WALKING OUT YOUR FRONT DOOR.

LIST ALL THE EXTRAVAGANT MATERIAL GOODS YOU'D BUY IF
YOU HAD UNLIMITED FUNDS.

LIST THE COMPONENTS OF YOUR PERFECT DAY.

LIST ALL THE THINGS THAT JUST DON'T WORK.

LIST THE BRAND NAMES YOU BUY AND SWEAR BY.

LIST THOSE PRODUCTS YOU'D ELIMINATE TO MAKE A BETTER WORLD.

LIST THE TOOLS YOU CAN'T LIVE WITHOUT.

LIST ALL THE MODES OF TRANSPORTATION YOU'VE TAKEN.

LIST THOSE REGULAR DAILY ITEMS YOU WISH YOU NEVER HAD TO BUY AGAIN.

_____

_____

_____

_____

_____

_____

_____

_____

_____

_____

_____

_____

_____

_____

_____

_____

_____

_____

_____

_____

_____

LIST THE THINGS YOU SCREAM AND MUTTER WHEN STUCK ON TELEPHONE HOLD.

LIST WHAT ITEMS OF MODERN TECHNOLOGY HAVE MOST SHAPED YOUR LIFE.

LIST WHAT'S CONSISTENTLY IN YOUR GARBAGE.

LIST ALL THE GREETINGS YOU'VE USED TO ANSWER YOUR TELEPHONE.

LIST THE BEST GIFTS YOU'VE EVER BEEN GIVEN.

LIST ALL THE THINGS YOU'VE LENT THAT HAVE COME BACK BROKEN.

LIST ALL THE ITEMS IN YOUR WALLET.

LIST THE THINGS YOU THINK YOU CAN'T LIVE WITHOUT.

List the first thoughts that run through your mind the moment you get up.

_____

_____

_____

_____

_____

_____

_____

_____

_____

_____

_____

_____

_____

_____

_____

_____

_____

_____

_____

_____

LIST THE FOOD THAT'S ALWAYS LEFT IN YOUR REFRIGERATOR AFTER EVERYTHING ELSE IS EATEN.

LIST THE FANTASTIC PRANKS YOU'VE SUCCESSFULLY PULLED OFF.

LIST ALL THE ACCIDENTS YOU'VE BEEN IN.

LIST WHAT'S IN YOUR GLOVE COMPARTMENT.

LIST THE SECRET OBJECTS, WRITING, PAPERS YOU HOPE NO
ONE EVER UNCOVERS.

LIST ALL THE FEARS YOU HAVE WHEN YOU WAKE UP IN THE MORNING.

_____

_____

_____

_____

_____

_____

_____

_____

_____

_____

_____

_____

_____

_____

_____

_____

_____

_____

_____

BUSINESS

LIST ALL THE TIPS PEOPLE HAVE GIVEN YOU TO HELP YOU DO BUSINESS BETTER.

_____

_____

_____

_____

_____

_____

_____

_____

_____

_____

_____

_____

_____

_____

_____

_____

_____

_____

_____

_____

LIST THE TIMES YOU FELL INTO A BAD DEAL.

LIST ALL THE CONTRACTS YOU'VE SIGNED.

LIST THOSE PROJECTS YOU PUT OFF TIME AND TIME AGAIN.

LIST THOSE RISKS YOU'D LIKE TO TAKE BUT ARE AFRAID TO.

_____

_____

_____

_____

_____

_____

_____

_____

_____

_____

_____

_____

_____

_____

_____

_____

_____

_____

_____

_____

LIST ALL THE PEOPLE YOU'D LOVE TO SUE.

_____

_____

_____

_____

_____

_____

_____

_____

_____

_____

_____

_____

_____

_____

_____

_____

_____

_____

_____

_____

LIST FIVE POSITIONS OR PROJECTS YOU WISH YOU WERE
PRESENTLY INVOLVED WITH.

_____

_____

_____

_____

_____

_____

_____

_____

_____

_____

_____

_____

_____

_____

_____

_____

_____

_____

_____

LIST WHAT YOU'D LIKE TO SHOUT OUT LOUD TO YOUR BOSS OR CO-WORKERS.

LIST THE THINGS YOU'D RATHER BE DOING WHEN YOU ARE AT WORK.

_____

_____

_____

_____

_____

_____

_____

_____

_____

_____

_____

_____

_____

_____

_____

_____

_____

_____

_____

_____

LIST ALL THE WARNINGS YOU'VE HEARD ABOUT THE EVILS OF BUSINESS.

LIST THE EARLY JOBS YOU HAD AS A CHILD, TEENAGER, OR YOUNG ADULT.

LIST ALL THE IDIOTIC THINGS YOU'VE DONE FOR MONEY.

LIST THE CHECKS YOU WRITE EVERY MONTH THAT YOU ARE LOATH TO SIGN.

LIST ALL THOSE HARE-BRAINED GET-RICH SCHEMES THAT YOU
NEVER DID ANYTHING ABOUT.

_____

_____

_____

_____

_____

_____

_____

_____

_____

_____

_____

_____

_____

_____

_____

_____

_____

_____

_____

LIST THE OCCUPATIONS YOU FIND DESPICABLE.

LIST ALL THE PEOPLE WHO OWE YOU MONEY.

LIST THE TOP CHANGES YOU WOULD MAKE AT YOUR COMPANY.

LIST THE NAMES OF ALL YOUR PAST BOSSES.

LIST THE TIMES YOU'VE CHEATED AND GOTTEN AWAY WITH IT.

_____

_____

_____

_____

_____

_____

_____

_____

_____

_____

_____

_____

_____

_____

_____

_____

_____

_____

_____

_____

_____

_____

LIST THE DANGEROUS THINGS YOU HAVE DONE FOR MONEY.

LIST ALL THE TIMES YOU'VE HIT THE JACKPOT.

LIST THE BUSINESSES YOU WISH YOU PRESENTLY OWNED.

List the ways you make it through a tough business day.

_____

_____

_____

_____

_____

_____

_____

_____

_____

_____

_____

_____

_____

_____

_____

_____

_____

_____

_____

LIST THE MAJOR PROJECTS, BUSINESSES, OR VENTURES THAT
ARE MAKING YOU MONEY RIGHT NOW.

List the moves you wish you could change to rewrite your business history.

_____

_____

_____

_____

_____

_____

_____

_____

_____

_____

_____

_____

_____

_____

_____

_____

_____

_____

_____

STARTING TOMORROW YOU ARE THE CEO AT YOUR PLACE OF WORK. LIST WHO WOULD GO OR STAY, AND ALL OTHER CHANGES NEEDED.

_____

_____

_____

_____

_____

_____

_____

_____

_____

_____

_____

_____

_____

_____

_____

_____

_____

_____

_____

_____

_____

LIST YOUR MOST VALUED BUSINESS TIPS, TERMS, LESSONS, AND WEAPONS.

LIST THE IDEAS, PROJECTS, OR JOBS THAT ARE IN YOUR THOUGHTS AT THE PRESENT TIME.

CHANGE

LIST ALL THOSE EVENTS YOU WENT INTO WITH DOUBT THAT TURNED OUT SURPRISINGLY WELL.

_____

_____

_____

_____

_____

_____

_____

_____

_____

_____

_____

_____

_____

_____

_____

_____

_____

_____

_____

LIST THE PEOPLE YOU'LL ALWAYS INCLUDE IN YOUR WILL.

LIST THE WAYS YOU HAVE CHANGED FOR THE BETTER.

LIST THE THINGS YOU MUST DO BEFORE YOU DIE.

_____

_____

_____

_____

_____

_____

_____

_____

_____

_____

_____

_____

_____

_____

_____

_____

_____

_____

_____

_____

_____

_____

LIST THE PLACES YOU'VE VISITED THAT HAVE ALTERED YOUR
VIEW OF THE WORLD.

_____

_____

_____

_____

_____

_____

_____

_____

_____

_____

_____

_____

_____

_____

_____

_____

_____

_____

_____

_____

LIST THE MOST EXHILARATING EXPERIENCES YOU'VE EVER HAD.

List the transitions in your life that taught you the most.

_____

_____

_____

_____

_____

_____

_____

_____

_____

_____

_____

_____

_____

_____

_____

_____

_____

_____

_____

_____

LIST THE ATTITUDES AND HABITS YOU'VE HAD TO GIVE UP TO GET THROUGH LIFE.

LIST THE BELIEFS YOU'D GO OUT ON A LIMB FOR.

_____

_____

_____

_____

_____

_____

_____

_____

_____

_____

_____

_____

_____

_____

_____

_____

_____

_____

_____

_____

LIST THE RIVERS YOU'VE CROSSED.

LIST THE MAJOR BETRAYALS IN YOUR LIFE.

LIST THE QUALITIES YOU FEEL MAKE YOU DIFFERENT AS AN ADULT THAN A CHILD.

LIST ALL THE ELEMENTS IN A PERFECT VACATION.

_____

_____

_____

_____

_____

_____

_____

_____

_____

_____

_____

_____

_____

_____

_____

_____

_____

_____

_____

_____

_____

LIST THE BIGGEST TURNING POINTS IN YOUR LIFE.

LIST ANY CLOSE ENCOUNTERS WITH DEATH.

LIST THE WAYS YOU SABOTAGE YOURSELF FROM GETTING WHAT YOU WANT.

_____

_____

_____

_____

_____

_____

_____

_____

_____

_____

_____

_____

_____

_____

_____

_____

_____

_____

_____

_____

LIST ALL THE TIMES YOU'VE GONE OFF THE BEATEN PATH.

LIST HOW YOU'D LIKE TO CHANGE YOUR OUTER LIFE RIGHT NOW.

_____

_____

_____

_____

_____

_____

_____

_____

_____

_____

_____

_____

_____

_____

_____

_____

_____

_____

_____

_____

_____

_____

_____

LIST HOW YOU'D LIKE TO CHANGE YOUR INNER LIFE RIGHT NOW.

LIST ALL THE TIMES YOU'VE FALLEN FLAT ON YOUR FACE.

LIST SOME OF THE PEOPLE WHO HAVE REALLY CHANGED YOUR LIFE.

LIST THE DISASTERS YOU'VE SURVIVED.

List all the phone calls that changed your life.

_____

_____

_____

_____

_____

_____

_____

_____

_____

_____

_____

_____

_____

_____

_____

_____

_____

_____

_____

_____

LIST YOUR MENU FOR YOUR LAST SUPPER.

LIST THE MAJOR LOSSES YOU'VE SURVIVED IN YOUR LIFE.

LIST THE MAJOR CHANGES YOU FEEL YOU NEED TO MAKE IN YOUR LIFE RIGHT NOW.

LIST ALL THE MENTORS, DEAD OR ALIVE, YOU WISH YOU COULD HAVE ACCESS TO.

_____

_____

_____

_____

_____

_____

_____

_____

_____

_____

_____

_____

_____

_____

_____

_____

_____

_____

_____

_____

_____

_____

CULTURE

LIST HOW YOU'VE CONTRIBUTED TO THE WELFARE OF THE PLANET.

_____

_____

_____

_____

_____

_____

_____

_____

_____

_____

_____

_____

_____

_____

_____

_____

_____

_____

_____

_____

_____

List how you try to be ecologically sound.

LIST HOW YOU FEEL CONNECTED TO OTHER PEOPLE AROUND THE WORLD.

List the patriotic gestures you've made.

_____

_____

_____

_____

_____

_____

_____

_____

_____

_____

_____

_____

_____

_____

_____

_____

_____

_____

_____

_____

_____

_____

LIST ALL THE CELEBRITIES YOU'D LIKE TO SOCK IN THE FACE.

LIST ALL THE CELEBRITIES YOU'D LIKE TO HAVE SEX WITH.

List the news you've made.

_____

_____

_____

_____

_____

_____

_____

_____

_____

_____

_____

_____

_____

_____

_____

_____

_____

_____

_____

LIST THE WAYS THE GOVERNMENT LIES TO YOU.

LIST ALL THE MAGAZINES YOU SUBSCRIBE TO.

LIST ALL YOUR FAVORITE RADIO STATIONS, FROM CHILDHOOD ON.

LIST THE READING MATERIAL IN YOUR BATHROOM.

LIST THE MOVIES YOU'VE SEEN THAT WERE REALLY WORTH TWO HOURS OF YOUR LIFE.

_____

_____

_____

_____

_____

_____

_____

_____

_____

_____

_____

_____

_____

_____

_____

_____

_____

_____

_____

_____

LIST THE CULTURAL SPOTS YOU'VE VISITED THAT MOVE YOU SO MUCH YOU ARE SPEECHLESS.

LIST THE TV EXPERIENCES THAT TOUCHED YOU MOST DEEPLY.

LIST THOSE RESTRICTIONS, FROM STOP SIGNS TO GRAVITY, THAT YOU CAN'T STAND LIVING WITH.

_____

_____

_____

_____

_____

_____

_____

_____

_____

_____

_____

_____

_____

_____

_____

_____

_____

_____

_____

_____

_____

LIST ALL THE TIMES YOU GOT IN TROUBLE WITH THE LAW.

_____

_____

_____

_____

_____

_____

_____

_____

_____

_____

_____

_____

_____

_____

_____

_____

_____

_____

_____

_____

_____

_____

LIST ALL THE SONGS YOU KNOW BY HEART.

LIST WHAT YOU BELIEVE EXISTS IN OUTER SPACE.

LIST WHAT YOU DREAD ABOUT CHRISTMAS OR HANUKKAH.

LIST THE PIECES OF YOUR FAVORITE OUTFIT.

List the way you feel when a car alarm goes off.

_____

_____

_____

_____

_____

_____

_____

_____

_____

_____

_____

_____

_____

_____

_____

_____

_____

_____

LIST THE LINES YOU'RE SICK OF WAITING IN.

LIST THE CONTESTS AND AWARDS YOU'VE WON.

_____

_____

_____

_____

_____

_____

_____

_____

_____

_____

_____

_____

_____

_____

_____

_____

_____

_____

_____

_____

_____

_____

_____

LIST THE MUSIC THAT CHANGED YOUR LIFE.

LIST THE QUOTES YOU FIND YOURSELF SPOUTING.

LIST THOSE POSSESSIONS YOU ARE PROUDEST OF.

List all those pieces of culture you would really want on your desert island.

LIST ALL THE THINGS THAT COULD HAPPEN TO YOU WHEN YOU PARK IN AN UNDERGROUND STRUCTURE.

MEN AND WOMEN

LIST ALL THE PEOPLE YOU'VE HURT THAT YOU'D LIKE TO UNHURT.

LIST THE STRANGEST PEOPLE YOU'VE MET.

LIST THOSE FEATURES THAT GRAB YOUR ATTENTION WHEN A MAN OR A WOMAN WALKS BY.

LIST WHAT YOU LIKE TO DO AFTER SEX.

LIST THE PEOPLE YOU LOVE.

LIST THE NICEST THINGS ANYONE EVER DID FOR YOU.

_____

_____

_____

_____

_____

_____

_____

_____

_____

_____

_____

_____

_____

_____

_____

_____

_____

_____

_____

_____

_____

_____

LIST ALL THE IDIOTIC THINGS YOU HAVE DONE FOR LOVE.

LIST THE HEROIC THINGS YOU HAVE DONE FOR LOVE.

LIST THE WORDS YOU LOVE TO HAVE WHISPERED IN YOUR EAR.

LIST THE WAY JEALOUSY HAS RUINED YOUR LIFE.

LIST THE PEOPLE YOU'D LIKE TO WEED OUT FROM YOUR LIFE.

LIST THE PEOPLE YOU'VE TOLD OFF IN THE LAST YEAR.

LIST ALL THE RELATIONSHIP PROBLEMS YOU ARE TIRED OF
HEARING ABOUT FROM YOUR FRIENDS.

List what values you need in a lover, significant other, or mate.

_____

_____

_____

_____

_____

_____

_____

_____

_____

_____

_____

_____

_____

_____

_____

_____

_____

_____

_____

LIST THE BOYS OR GIRLS YOU WENT STEADY WITH AND THE
SENTIMENTAL ITEMS THEY GAVE YOU OR YOU SAVED.

LIST THE ONES THAT GOT AWAY.

LIST ALL THE TYPICAL REASONS YOU END A RELATIONSHIP.

LIST WHAT'S WRONG WITH WOMEN.

LIST WHAT'S WRONG WITH MEN.

LIST WHAT YOU WOULD CHANGE IN YOUR LOVER(S) RIGHT NOW.

LIST WHAT YOU WOULD SAY IF THE ONE WHO GOT AWAY
SHOWED UP IN YOUR ROOM.

LIST THE THINGS YOU WILL NOT TOLERATE NO MATTER WHAT THE COST.

LIST YOUR SUREFIRE SEXY MOVES AND LINES.

LIST THE THINGS YOU'VE DONE TO GET NOTICED.

_____

_____

_____

_____

_____

_____

_____

_____

_____

_____

_____

_____

_____

_____

_____

_____

_____

_____

_____

_____

_____

_____

_____

List the traits you require in a partner for true intimacy.

LIST ALL THE EXCUSES YOU'VE USED TO GET OUT OF DATES OR
APPOINTMENTS.

LIST THE QUALITIES YOU'D LIKE TO CHANGE IN YOUR LOVER OR SPOUSE.

LIST ALL THE PEOPLE YOU AREN'T TALKING TO ANYMORE.

LIST THE REASONS FOR GETTING MARRIED.

LIST YOUR FEARS ABOUT WHAT MIGHT HAPPEN IF YOU REALLY OPEN UP YOUR HEART.

_____

_____

_____

_____

_____

_____

_____

_____

_____

_____

_____

_____

_____

_____

_____

_____

_____

_____

_____

_____

_____

_____

LIST WHAT YOU WOULD DO DIFFERENTLY TO MAKE THE NEXT LOVE CONNECTION WORK.

LIST THE REASONS YOU HAVEN'T MET THE MAN OR WOMAN OF YOUR DREAMS.

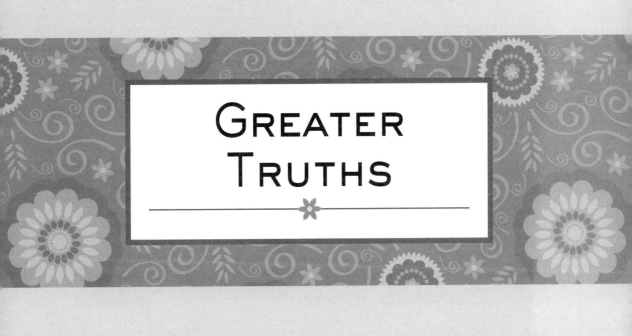

GREATER
TRUTHS

LIST THE REAL REASONS YOU ARE INSPIRED TO STAY ALIVE.

LIST THE WORDS THAT TOUCH YOUR SOUL.

LIST THE TIMES YOU SAID YES WHEN YOU WISH YOU'D SAID NO.

LIST ALL THE PLACES YOU'VE BEEN THAT MADE YOU FEEL
IMMORTAL, MOVED TO TEARS, OR OMNIPOTENT.

LIST THE TIMES YOU HAVE CONSCIOUSLY ENDANGERED YOUR LIFE.

_____

_____

_____

_____

_____

_____

_____

_____

_____

_____

_____

_____

_____

_____

_____

_____

_____

_____

LIST THE THINGS YOU PRESENTLY FIND YOURSELF PRAYING FOR.

LIST THOSE UNANSWERED QUESTIONS THAT HAVE BEEN PLAGUING YOU SINCE CHILDHOOD.

LIST YOUR LIFE'S MAIN REGRETS.

List the epitaphs you might like on your tombstone.

LIST ALL THE TIMES YOU "KNEW" SOMETHING BUT DIDN'T TRUST YOUR INTUITION.

LIST THE THINGS YOU CAN PROVE ARE TRUE.

LIST THE WAYS YOU'VE BEEN AFFECTED BY A HIGHER POWER.

LIST YOUR LUCKY CHARMS.

LIST ALL THE THINGS YOU JUST DON'T WANT TO THINK ABOUT.

_____
_____
_____
_____
_____
_____
_____
_____
_____
_____
_____
_____
_____
_____
_____
_____
_____
_____
_____
_____
_____
_____

LIST ALL THE EXPERIENCES THAT GIVE YOU GOOSE BUMPS.

LIST ALL THE PRAYERS, SAYINGS, AND CHANTS YOU'VE BEEN
TAUGHT THAT MAKE YOU FEEL BETTER.

_____

_____

_____

_____

_____

_____

_____

_____

_____

_____

_____

_____

_____

_____

_____

_____

_____

_____

_____

_____

_____

LIST WHAT HEALS YOUR ACHING SOUL.

LIST ANY MIRACLES YOU'VE SEEN HAPPEN.

LIST ALL THE MYSTERIOUS THINGS YOU'VE SEEN IN THE DARK.

LIST ALL THE OCCASIONS YOU'VE SPOTTED SOMETHING
UNIDENTIFIABLE IN THE NIGHT SKY.

LIST THOSE MOMENTS IN NATURE THAT REMIND YOU OF YOUR CONNECTION TO THE "BIG PICTURE."

_____

_____

_____

_____

_____

_____

_____

_____

_____

_____

_____

_____

_____

_____

_____

_____

_____

_____

LIST THE MOST IMPORTANT TURNING POINTS IN YOUR LIFE.

_____

_____

_____

_____

_____

_____

_____

_____

_____

_____

_____

_____

_____

_____

_____

_____

_____

_____

_____

_____

_____

_____

HEALTH

LIST ALL THE THINGS YOU CAN DO WITH YOUR EYES CLOSED.

List all the stuff in your medicine cabinet.

List the ways you live ecologically in your home.

LIST THE THINGS YOU DO THAT YOU CONSIDER BAD, WRONG, OR UNACCEPTABLE.

LIST THE FOODS YOU'D EAT IF GUARANTEED YOU WOULDN'T GET FAT.

List those body parts you'd love to change or replace.

LIST THE DRUGS YOU'VE TRIED.

List all the self-improvement techniques you've experimented with.

LIST THE WAYS YOU TREAT A COLD.

LIST WHAT YOU KNOW ABOUT THE HUMAN BODY.

LIST THE PHYSICAL AILMENTS YOU ARE TIRED OF HAVING.

_____

_____

_____

_____

_____

_____

_____

_____

_____

_____

_____

_____

_____

_____

_____

_____

_____

_____

_____

_____

_____

_____

LIST YOUR FAVORITE COOKING INGREDIENTS.

LIST ALL THE THINGS YOU DO TO STOP HICCUPPING.

List what you hear when you get very quiet.

LIST ALL THE THOUGHTS AND ACTIVITIES IN YOUR DAY THAT PHYSICALLY DRAIN YOU.

LIST ALL THE HABITS YOU SIMPLY CAN'T BREAK.

LIST WHAT YOU DO TO RESTORE YOUR SOUL.

List your recurring nightmares.

LIST THE PARTS OF YOUR BODY THAT MAKE YOU FEEL LIKE "YOU."

LIST ALL THE HALLUCINATIONS YOU'VE HAD.

LIST COMMON PHYSICAL PROBLEMS YOU USE TO GET SYMPATHY.

List the signs of aging you see in your mirror.

LIST ALL THE BOGUS HEALTH FADS YOU'VE TRIED OR
WANTED TO DO.

_____

_____

_____

_____

_____

_____

_____

_____

_____

_____

_____

_____

_____

_____

_____

_____

_____

_____

_____

LIST ALL THE PLACES ON YOUR BODY YOU LOVE BEING TOUCHED.

_____

_____

_____

_____

_____

_____

_____

_____

_____

_____

_____

_____

_____

_____

_____

_____

_____

_____

LIST HOW YOU BEAT INSOMNIA.

_____

_____

_____

_____

_____

_____

_____

_____

_____

_____

_____

_____

_____

_____

_____

_____

_____

_____

_____

_____

LIST ALL THE HABITS YOU'VE SUCCESSFULLY KICKED.

LIST THE NATURAL PHENOMENA THAT REALLY UNNERVE YOU.

LIST YOUR ADDICTIONS.

_____

_____

_____

_____

_____

_____

_____

_____

_____

_____

_____

_____

_____

_____

_____

_____

_____

_____

_____

_____

_____

LIST ALL THE "IDENTIFIABLE MARKS" UNIQUE TO YOU ALONE.

LIST THE RITUALS YOU DO BEFORE GOING TO BED.

GROWING UP

LIST THE NAMES OF ALL YOUR PETS, FROM CHILDHOOD UNTIL TODAY.

_____

_____

_____

_____

_____

_____

_____

_____

_____

_____

_____

_____

_____

_____

_____

_____

_____

_____

_____

_____

LIST ALL YOUR FAVORITE LOST ITEMS.

List the sights, smells, and sounds you remember from your grandparents' house.

_____

_____

_____

_____

_____

_____

_____

_____

_____

_____

_____

_____

_____

_____

_____

_____

_____

_____

_____

_____

_____

LIST THE TOYS, CLOTHES, AND OTHER ITEMS YOU WISH YOU COULD HAVE SAVED FROM YOUR CHILDHOOD.

LIST THE TEACHERS THAT CHANGED YOUR LIFE.

LIST THE EXPERIENCES YOU HAD AS A CHILD THAT YOU KNEW WERE TRULY SIGNIFICANT.

LIST THE LIFE-ALTERING MAGICAL TIMES YOU HAD ALONE.

List what was under your bed as a child.

LIST THE BEST STUFF YOUR PARENTS TAUGHT YOU ABOUT LIVING LIFE.

LIST THE THINGS YOU USED TO DO WHEN YOU GOT HOME
FROM SCHOOL.

LIST THE FOODS, CANDY, AND OTHER TREATS YOU LOVED TO SNACK ON.

_____

_____

_____

_____

_____

_____

_____

_____

_____

_____

_____

_____

_____

_____

_____

_____

_____

_____

_____

_____

LIST THE WARNINGS AND OLD WIVES' TALES YOU WERE TAUGHT.

LIST ALL THE DETAILS YOU CAN REMEMBER ABOUT YOUR
CHILDHOOD BEDROOM.

LIST WHAT YOU COULDN'T STAND ABOUT THE WAY YOU LOOKED AS A TEENAGER.

_____

_____

_____

_____

_____

_____

_____

_____

_____

_____

_____

_____

_____

_____

_____

_____

_____

_____

_____

_____

_____

LIST THE FADS YOU EMBRACED WHILE GROWING UP.

LIST ALL THE OBJECTS YOU WISH YOU HAD FROM YOUR
PARENTS' LIVING ROOM.

_____

_____

_____

_____

_____

_____

_____

_____

_____

_____

_____

_____

_____

_____

_____

_____

_____

_____

_____

LIST THE THINGS YOU SAW OR OVERHEARD THAT NO ONE KNEW ABOUT.

LIST THE TIMES YOU DID SOMETHING UNETHICAL THAT YOU
NEVER TOLD ANYONE ABOUT.

LIST THE SCARY CREATURES YOU SAW IN YOUR ROOM
AT NIGHT.

_____

_____

_____

_____

_____

_____

_____

_____

_____

_____

_____

_____

_____

_____

_____

_____

_____

_____

LIST WHO YOU WANTED TO BE LIKE WHEN YOU GREW UP.

List what you feared about becoming an adult.

_____

_____

_____

_____

_____

_____

_____

_____

_____

_____

_____

_____

_____

_____

_____

_____

_____

_____

_____

_____

_____

LIST THOSE FAVORITE THINGS, COLLECTIONS, AND LUCKY CHARMS YOU TREASURED.

LIST THE TIMES YOU WERE MOST EMBARRASSED.

_____

_____

_____

_____

_____

_____

_____

_____

_____

_____

_____

_____

_____

_____

_____

_____

_____

_____

_____

_____

_____

_____

_____

List all the beasts, characters, and creatures you were on Halloween.

List all the rumors you started.

_____

_____

_____

_____

_____

_____

_____

_____

_____

_____

_____

_____

_____

_____

_____

_____

_____

_____

SUDDENLY . . .

SUDDENLY YOU'VE ARRIVED ON JUPITER. LIST THE THINGS
YOU CAN'T LIVE WITHOUT.

SUDDENLY YOU'VE BEEN GRANTED LUNCH WITH GOD. LIST YOUR GRIEVANCES.

_____

_____

_____

_____

_____

_____

_____

_____

_____

_____

_____

_____

_____

_____

_____

_____

_____

_____

_____

_____

SUDDENLY YOUR HOUSE IS ON FIRE. LIST THE STUFF YOU'D
GRAB TO SAVE.

_____

_____

_____

_____

_____

_____

_____

_____

_____

_____

_____

_____

_____

_____

_____

_____

_____

_____

_____

_____

SUDDENLY YOU POSSESS THE POWER TO BRING BACK
INDIVIDUALS FROM THE PAST. LIST WHO YOU FEEL WE NEED
ON EARTH RIGHT NOW.

SUDDENLY YOU CAN FORESEE THE FUTURE. LIST WHAT BIG
CHANGES WILL TAKE PLACE IN THE NEXT TWENTY-FIVE YEARS.

_____

_____

_____

_____

_____

_____

_____

_____

_____

_____

_____

_____

_____

_____

_____

_____

_____

_____

_____

_____

_____

_____

SUDDENLY YOU CAN TALK TO ANIMALS. LIST THE ONES YOU WANT TO CONVERSE WITH AND WHY.

SUDDENLY YOU ARE INVISIBLE. LIST WHERE YOU'D GO AND
WHAT YOU WOULD DO.

SUDDENLY YOU ARE AS THIN AS YOU WANT. LIST WHAT WOULD HAPPEN NOW.

SUDDENLY YOU CAN REWRITE HISTORY. LIST WHAT EVENTS YOU WOULD CHANGE AND HOW.

_____

_____

_____

_____

_____

_____

_____

_____

_____

_____

_____

_____

_____

_____

_____

_____

_____

_____

_____

_____

_____

SUDDENLY YOU CAN RE-CREATE YOUR CHILDHOOD. LIST WHAT EXPERIENCES YOU WOULD MAKE COME OUT DIFFERENTLY.

SUDDENLY YOU HAVE BEEN GRANTED A PRIVATE MEETING WITH THE PRESIDENT OF THE UNITED STATES. LIST WHAT TRUTHS YOU'D WANT TO UNCOVER.

SUDDENLY YOU CAN COMMUNICATE SAFELY WITH ALIENS. LIST THE SECRETS OF THE UNIVERSE YOU'D LIKE TO UNCOVER.

SUDDENLY, WHILE DRIVING AROUND TOWN, A CAR CUTS IN
FRONT OF YOU, ALMOST CAUSING A BAD ACCIDENT. LIST ALL
THE THINGS YOU'D LIKE TO DO TO THE CARELESS DRIVER.

SUDDENLY YOU HAVE FIVE MILLION DOLLARS THAT YOU MUST GIVE AWAY. LIST THE LUCKY RECIPIENTS.

SUDDENLY YOU CAN ELIMINATE INDIVIDUALS YOU FEEL ARE
A PROBLEM ON THE PLANET. YOU WILL NOT GET IN TROUBLE.
LIST THEM.

SUDDENLY YOU CAN TURN BACK TIME. LIST THE YEAR YOU
WOULD RETURN TO AND ALL THE EVENTS YOU WOULD CHANGE.

_____

_____

_____

_____

_____

_____

_____

_____

_____

_____

_____

_____

_____

_____

_____

_____

_____

_____

_____

_____

_____